ABOUT MAGIC READERS

ABDO continues its commitment to quality books with the nonfiction Magic Readers series. This series includes three levels of books to help students progress to being independent readers while learning factual information. Different levels are intended to reflect the stages of reading in the early grades, helping to select the best level for each individual student.

level 1

Level 1: Books with short sentences and familiar words or patterns to share with children who are beginning to understand how letters and sounds go together.

level 2

Level 2: Books with longer words and sentences and more complex language patterns with less repetition for progressing readers who are practicing common words and letter sounds.

level 3

Level 3: Books with more developed language and vocabulary for transitional readers who are using strategies to figure out unknown words and are ready to learn information more independently.

These nonfiction readers are aligned with the Common Core State Standards progression of literacy, following the sequence of skills and increasing the difficulty of language while engaging the curious minds of young children. These books also reflect the increasing importance of reading informational material in the early grades. They encourage children to read for fun and to learn!

Hannah E. Tolles, MA Reading Specialist

www.abdopublishing.com

Published by Magic Wagon, a division of ABDO, PO Box 398166, Minneapolis, Minnesota 55439. Copyright © 2015 by Abdo Consulting Group, Inc. International copyrights reserved in all countries. No part of this book may be reproduced in any form without written permission from the publisher. Magic Readers™ is a trademark and logo of Magic Wagon.

Printed in the United States of America, North Mankato, Minnesota.
042014
092014

Cover Photo: Thinkstock
Interior Photos: Thinkstock

Written and edited by Rochelle Baltzer, Heidi M. D. Elston,
    Megan M. Gunderson, and Bridget O'Brien
Designed and illustrated by Candice Keimig

Library of Congress Cataloging-in-Publication Data

Baltzer, Rochelle, 1982-
  Dolphins.
      pages cm. -- (Magic readers. Level 1)
   "Written and edited by Rochelle Baltzer, Heidi Elston, Megan M. Gunderson,
   and Bridget O'Brien, designed and illustrated by Candice Keimig."--T.p. verso.
   ISBN 978-1-62402-066-7
1. Dolphins--Juvenile literature. I. Keimig, Candice,
illustrator. II. Title.
   QL737.C432B365 2014
   599.53--dc23
                       2014001055

Magic Readers

level 1

Dolphins

By Rochelle Baltzer
Illustrated photos by Candice Keimig

Magic Readers

An Imprint of Magic Wagon
www.abdopublishing.com

This is a dolphin.

It is a bottlenose dolphin.

Dolphins live in salt water.

The water is warm.

A dolphin has smooth skin.

It is gray.

A dolphin has a fin.

fin

It has a tail too.

tail

A dolphin needs air.

It can see and hear and feel.

A dolphin has a beak.

beak

It has small teeth in its beak.

A dolphin can catch fish.

It can stand on its tail.

Dolphins are smart.

They click to talk.

19

A dolphin swims fast.

It swims with its pod.

Dolphins can play.

They can jump in the air.

Dolphins look happy!